AUTHENTIC

Charleston, SC
www.PalmettoPublishing.com

AUTHENTIC
Copyright © 2023 by Ciara Dove

Visit me on the web!
www.CiaraDove.com

All rights reserved

Hardcover ISBN: 979-8-8229-2493-2
Paperback ISBN: 979-8-8229-2494-9
eBook ISBN: 979-8-8229-3279-1

AUTHENTIC

Poetry in the Raw...

Dedicated to...

The woman that gave me life
and the ability to do this.
I seek to continue to make you proud.
Mommie,
I love you and miss you so much.

#3 of The Margo6
- Cici

Prologue

Thinking about all the things that needed to be done to get this first book going was such a tedious task. A task that I've put off for far too long. I believe in authenticity, and the beauty of words spoken with a stroke of a pen (pencil in some cases). There is nothing like seeing the process of writing poetry in its rawest form. I'd like to take you to a few places in my mind, mostly from my point of view and some from others; but ALL my words.

There are haikus, and some poems that'll have numbers 1-4 next to them. This just means that is the order in which you are to read them, so it makes sense with the previous quatrain. Other types of poems you will encounter are in acrostic form; that reads a word, name, or title vertically.

I think poetry should be fun to read, all while making you laugh, cry, and remember things, people, and times in your life. My manuscript is legible for the most part, so I ask that you keep an open mind. A typed version has been added to each poem for your reading ease. This is my first ever published work, so let's have fun with it.

Without further ado, please allow me to take you
through the many journeys of my thoughts.
This is just the beginning.

Enjoy!

The Essence

This poetry book is not a by-the-book kind of book.

◇ Mark your favorites here, as you go!

Title	**Page**
◇ My Heart's Desire	3
◇ Love For MJ	5
◇ He Is…	7
◇ Eternal Togetherness	9
◇ Life or Something Like It	11
◇ Angry Woman	13
◇ Exploration	15
◇ Special	17
◇ Dead End Relationship	19
◇ Just Let Go	23
◇ Incompatible	27
◇ No Regrets	29
◇ Will You Miss Me?	31
◇ Part of My Character	33
◇ I Want to Read Your Thoughts	35
◇ Curiosity	37
◇ #1 Fan	39
◇ Juvenile	41
◇ Mommie, Don't Go	43
◇ Mommie's Secret	47
◇ The Funnies of Love	49
◇ Through the Mother's Eyes	51
◇ Through the Unborn Child's Eyes	55
◇ Missing Angel	59
◇ Mc Lovin'	61
◇ What's Next?	63
◇ Letting Go	65

◇ Patience I. 67
◇ Your Loss 69
◇ Do Me Right 73
◇ Vain 75
◇ Stubborn Mama 77
◇ The Blame Game 79
◇ Love Conquers Addiction 81
◇ Survival Through Song 83
◇ Time is of the Essence 85
◇ You Should Be Here 87
◇ Un-Supportive 89
◇ My Prerogative I. 91
◇ My Prerogative II. 93
◇ Suicide 95
◇ Where's Daddy? 97
◇ Happy Thoughts 99
◇ Judge Me Not 101
◇ Can't Get Right 103
◇ Be Firm 105
◇ Tell Me the Truth 107
◇ Deal With It 109
◇ I Miss Us 111
◇ Same Color in the Dark 113
◇ His Insecurity 115
◇ Too Little, Too Late 117
◇ Hell-Crazy Love 119
◇ The Distance I. 121
◇ Confessedly 123
◇ Don't Be… 125
◇ Karma 127
◇ She's Not Your Type 129
◇ Say You, Say Me 131
◇ Patience II. 133
Acknowledgements 135
About the Author 137

Poetry in the Raw...

10/1/08.   My Heart's Desire

Do I follow my heart's desire
Or do I follow my heart
I want to do my own thing now
So with one of them I have to part

My heart's desire is to find me
Find out who I am & what I stand for
Test the capacity of my capabilities
And find out what exactly life has in store

My heart's desire is to embark on new experiences
Go places I've never been & Do things I've never done
Meet people I never thought I'd meet
Perhaps even tan nude, under the blazing hot sun

My heart's desire is to go back to school
Be someone I thought I wouldn't
Take on new and exciting challenges
Prepare to do things I thought I couldn't

2

My Heart's Desire

Do I follow my heart's desire
Or do I follow my heart?
I want to do my own thing now
So with one of them I have to part

My heart's desire is to find me
Find out who I am and what I stand for
Test the capacity of my capabilities
And find out what exactly life has in store

My heart's desire is to embark on new experiences
Go places I've never been and do things I've never done
Meet people I never thought I'd meet
Perhaps even tan nude under the blazing hot sun

My heart's desire is to go back to school
Be someone I thought I wouldn't
Take on new and exciting challenges
Prepare to do things I thought I couldn't

2006

Love for MJ

Lonely is what I am going to feel without you around
for a week
Oath of sexual silence is what I'll take until I
feel your warm clasping love
Vivacious is what I'll be the next time I see you
Empty is what I am feeling inside and I haven't
even left yet

Forever always is what you will be in my heart
Overwhelmed is my mind with thoughts of you
Rainy shall be my days from the absence of you

Melancholy is my spirit until we meet again
Joyous it would be to see, feel, and hold you in
my arms again

4

Love For MJ

Lonely is what I am going to feel without you around for a week
Oath of sexual silence is what I'll take until I feel your warm clasping love
Vivacious is what I'll be the next time I see you
Empty is what I am feeling inside and I haven't even left yet

Forever always is what you will be in my heart
Overwhelmed is my mind with thoughts of you
Rainy shall be my days from the absence of you

Melancholy is my spirit until we meet again
Joyous it would be to see, feel, and hold you in my arms again

2/13/06

He Is...

multi-tasn is he
fond of me is he
Love of my life is he
Adorned by all is he

The yin to my yang he will be
my one and only he will be
Father of my child he will be
My husband to be you'll see... he will be

6

He Is...

Multi task is he
Fond of me is he
Love of my life is he
Adorned by all is he

The yin to my yang he will be
My one and only he will be
Father of my child he will be
My husband to be, you'll see…he will be

my head on your chest listening to the throb of
　　your heart beat
The rhythm, the sound as if it beats triple times
I look in your eyes and you look in mine so deep
The pleasure and pain of engagement still fresh
　　in my mind

The glisten in your eyes is what I long to wake
　　up to
With the soft touch of your fingertips in the
　　small of my back
I wish we could stay in bed forever to keep
　　our love fresh and new
Then reality sets in to the only thing we lack...

　　　Eternal Togetherness

Eternal Togetherness

My head on your chest listening to the throb of your heart beat
The rhythm, the sound as if it beats triple times
I look in your eyes and you look in mine so deep
The pleasure and pain of engagement still fresh in my mind

The glisten in your eyes is what I long to wake up to
With the soft touch of your fingertips in the small of my back
I wish we could stay in bed forever to keep our love fresh and new
Then reality sets in, to the only thing we lack…

(Eternal Togetherness)

Life or Something Like It

Learning experience
Illusion of one's portrayal of it
Fantasy of one's mind; visual of unrealization
Eclectic view of what people want you to see

Omitting the obvious to stick around for the
        convenience
Rebuilding the foundation of a broke down palace

Special is no one
Opposite is everyone
Moral support is what we all need
Even the stubborn ones
Total control is what we lack at times with
Hesitation to making the right decisions
Instantaneous results we get with
Nothing loss and no regrets
Glorious is the day

Life is not taught
It is learned
Kick out the negativity
Embrace the positivity

Ignore what you have no control of
Take ownership of what you do

Life or Something Like It

Learning experience
Illusion of one's portrayal of it
Fantasy of one's mind; visual of un-realization
Eclectic view of what people want you to see

Omitting the obvious to stick around for the convenience
Rebuilding the foundation of a broke down palace

Special is no one
Opposite is everyone
Moral support is what we all need
Even the stubborn ones
Total control is what we lack at times with
Hesitation to making the right decisions
Instantaneous results we get with
Nothing lost and no regrets
Glorious is the day

Life is not taught
It is learned
Kick out the negativity
Embrace more positivity

Ignore what you have no control of
Take ownership of what you do

8/23/06

Angry Woman

Ambitious and goal oriented is she
Never to be taken for a fool by anyone
Grave hopes and dreams for she and he
Ruined by one encounter with another woman
Yet she still survives ...

Wishful thinking of what could be between she and
           another
Obvious reasons of why he cannot commit
Moments of endearing acts of love toward each other
And yet the chances of them being a unit
Non-existent

Angry Woman

Ambitious and goal oriented is she
Never to be taken for a fool by anyone
Grave hopes and dreams for she and he
Ruined by one encounter with another woman
Yet she still survives…

Wishful thinking of what could be between she and another
Obvious reasons of why he cannot commit
Moments of endearing acts of love toward each other
And yet the chances of them being a unit
Non-existent…

11/14/00

Exploration

I want to take a tour of your body
From the top of your head
To kissing the ~~button~~ button of your nose
Then to the lobes of your ears
kiss your full lips so soft
My tongue massaging yours
Grazing the surface of your teeth
Work my way from your chin
To the sides of your neck
kiss and stroke your masculine chest
Then down your happy trail
Giving you my best performance
Squeeze your thighs
Tickle the back of your knees
~~Then back up~~
Then play with your toes and back up to the
top to start all over again

14

Exploration

I want to take a tour of your body
From the top of your head
To kissing the button of your nose
Then to the lobes of your ears
Kiss your full lips so soft
My tongue massaging yours
Grazing the surface of your teeth
Work my way from your chin
To the sides of your neck
Kiss and stroke your masculine chest
Then down your happy trail
Giving you my best performance
Squeeze your thighs
Tickle the back of your knees
Then play with your toes and back up to the top
to start all over again

11/14/06

Special

Spontaneous, because I love the way your slippery
      mind works
Prêt-â-porter, because I love the way you dress
Efficient in everything you do
Cordial, because you're always so sincere
Initially meant for me from our first encounter
Astonishing is your capabilities in the sack
Loving and luscious for the way you keep me
      pleasantly surprised

Special

Spontaneous, because I love the way your slippery mind works
Prêt-a-porter, because I love the way you dress
Efficient in everything you do
Cordial because you're always so sincere
Initially meant for me from our first encounter
Astonishing is your capabilities in the sack
Loving and luscious for the way you keep me pleasantly surprised

12/7/06

Dead End Relationship

I love you
And I know you love me
But you and I both know
What we want from each other will never be

You coming home to my sweet angelic face
Me anticipating you to eat the food I've prepared
Inhaling the sweet aroma of you favorite dish
You love it, it's good ... to nothing compared

So tell me exactly what is to come of this
now that it has been a few years
We see that we were meant for each other since the first
        kiss
I'm confused, I need to know why you still want me
        near

I've never doubted the love you have for me
Now it, I start to question
The feelings you express to me I know I'll some day see
I guess the day will come with our love child from
        conception

On the other hand, I feel like what you have I can't
        compete
I don't want to make things hard for you
Your family is what makes you whole and complete
And I'm just a fly by night that happens to be in love
        with you

Dead End Relationship

I love you
And I know you love me
But you and I both know
That what we want from each other will never be

You coming home to my sweet angelic face
Me anticipating you to eat the food I've prepared
Inhaling the sweet aroma of your favorite dish
You love it…it's good…to nothing compared

So tell me exactly what is to come of this
Now that it's been a few years
We see that we were meant for each other since the first kiss
I'm confused, I need to know why you still want me near

I've never doubted the love you have for me
Now it, I start to question
The feelings you express to me, I know I will someday see
I guess the day will come with our love child from conception

On the other hand, I feel like what you have I can't compete
I don't want to make things hard for you
Your family is what makes you whole and complete
And I'm just a fly by night that happens to be in love with you

Back to the matter at hand
Why am I still here?
You say nothing and have no demands
Still confused as to why you still want me near

There are times you make me feel like gold
The way you talk to me and treat me so well
But there are times you can be so cold
I can't do anything to turn things around while you dwell

Dwell on the argument from the night before
Dwell on the past tense
I thought your heart was an open door
Now I dwell while you keep me in suspense

Where has the love gone between you and me?
Because you're acting like a child right now
I guess it's dead along with chivalry and fidelity
Call me when you have the time, let me know if
     you still want me around

Back to the matter at hand
Why am I still here?
You say nothing and have no demands
Still confused as to why you still want me near

There are times where you make me feel like gold
The way you talk to me and treat me so well
But there are times you can be so cold
I can't do anything to turn things around while you dwell

Dwell on the argument from the night before
Dwell in the past tense
I thought your heart was an open door
Now I dwell, while you keep me in suspense

Where has the love gone between you and me?
Because you're acting like a child right now
I guess it's dead, along with chivalry and fidelity
Call me when you have the time; let me know if you still want
me around

Just Let Go

This isn't about you anymore
It hasn't been for a few years

You're being selfish and need to re-evaluate things
Things meaning yourself in particularly

Not everything has to be such a challenge
You make it this way because you're scared

Scared to live
Scared to grow
Scared to fail
Scared to let go and let flow

Never mind what everyone else says
Because they don't live your life

Stop asking questions
When you already know the answers

Stop being so hard on yourself
And live your life

Without the outside interference
Without the opinions of others
Without the love for another
Who can't love you like the other

Just Let Go

This isn't about you anymore
It hasn't been for a few years

You're being selfish and need to re-evaluate things
Things meaning yourself in particularly

Not everything has to be such a challenge
You make it this way because you're scared

Scared to live
Scared to grow
Scared to fail
Scared to let go and let flow

Never mind what everyone else says
Because they don't live your life

Stop asking questions
When you already know the answers

Stop being so hard on yourself
And live your life

Without the outside interference
Without the opinions of others
Without the love for another
Who can't love you like the other

Love you like you want to be loved
Treat you like you want to be treated
Devote the time and patience it takes to keep your attention
Stop being so stubborn and release some tension

I am you
So listen to me
I'm not fiction
I'm reality

I'm your conscience

continued

Love you like you want to be loved
Treat you like you want to be treated
Devote the time and patience it takes to keep your attention
Stop being so stubborn, and release some tension

I am you
So listen to me
I'm not fiction
I'm reality

I'm your conscience.

2007-1 God created you
He~~~~~~ created me
But he didn't create us
As an item to be

I don't think you're ready for this
As you are in a very vulnerable state right now
Looking for another woman should be last on your list
Especially one that isn't ready to settle down

Although I can not predict the future
I just don't ~~plan~~ plan on being the Rebound chick
To this relationship thing, I'm no amateur
Because these days I have a heart solid as a brick

I'm sure you may have what it takes to heal my soul
And possibly break through this barrier
How do you intend on achieving this with someone so
inconsolable
someone who can make you feel inferior

I'm not the one for you
As the truth tends to hurt
I know it's sad but true
However my intentions aren't to treat you like dirt

You're a really nice guy
But I'm afraid we can never be
my ~~other~~ intention was not to hurt your pride
But spare it from the likes of me

Incompatible

God created you
He created me
But he didn't create us
As an item to be

I don't think you're ready for this
As you are in a very vulnerable state right now
Looking for another woman should be last on your list
Especially one that isn't ready to settle down

Although I cannot predict the future
I just don't plan on being the rebound chick
To this relationship thing, I'm no amateur
Because these days I have a heart solid as a brick

I'm sure you may have what it takes to heal my soul
And possibly break through this barrier
How do you intend on achieving this with someone so inconsolable?
Someone who can make you feel inferior

I'm not the one for you
As the truth tends to hurt
I know it's sad but true
However, my intentions aren't to treat you like dirt

You're a really nice guy
But I'm afraid we can never be
My other intention was not to hurt your pride
But spare it from the likes of me

No Regrets

I wish we, can run away together
I wish we can do things in the open
I wish we can make love until the sun comes up
I wish I can sleep on your chest all night
I wish I can tell you "I love you" already
I wish I can get lost in your rapture
I wish I can have at least one of these wishes

I wish I could let you go
I wish I didn't lust you so much
I wish we never met
I wish this wasn't love.....but regret

Regret it is not
Regret it will never be
For the lust and love you have for me
Will stay in my heart for all eternity

28

No Regrets

I wish we can run away together
I wish we can do things in the open
I wish we can make love until the sun comes up
I wish I can sleep on your chest all night
I wish I can tell you, "I love you" already
I wish I can get lost in your rapture
I wish I could have at least one of these wishes

I wish I could let you go
I wish I didn't lust you so much
I wish we never met
I wish this wasn't love…but regret

Regret it is not
Regret it will never be
For the lust and love you have for me
Will stay in my heart for all eternity

Will you miss me

Will you miss me when I'm gone
Will you treasure each moment we've shared
Will you want for me when you're alone
Will you ever tell me how much you care

Tell me now or forever hold your peace
What it is exactly you want from me
Tell me now or forever hold your peace
Am I a want for you or am I a need

Because when all is said and done
You would have missed the opportunity
To tell me about what could have been
So will you miss me when I'm gone

Do you think you can love me like I want to be loved
Treat me like I want to be treated
Devote the time and patience it takes to keep my
        attention
Kiss me, hug me, hold me, and give me all your
        affection

Will You Miss Me?

Will you miss me when I'm gone?
Will you treasure each moment we've shared?
Will you want for me when you're alone?
Will you ever tell me how much you care?

Tell me now or forever hold your peace
What it is exactly you want from me?
Tell me now or forever hold your peace
Am I a want for you or am I a need?

Because when all is said and done
You would have missed the opportunity
To tell me about what could have been
So will you miss me when I'm gone?

Do you think you can love me like I want to be loved?
Treat me like I want to be treated

Devote the time and patience it takes to keep my attention
Kiss me, hug me, hold me, and give me all your affection

1/1/07 @ 12:58pm

Part of my Character

Will you stop!
Stop what?!
That damn laughing!
Sorry you can't shut me up

① This is me
③ This is my personality
② I thought you knew
④ The one thing you can't subdue

Part of My Character

Will you stop!
Stop what?
That damn laughing!
Sorry you can't shut me up

This is me
I thought you knew
This is my personality
The one thing you can't subdue

11/9/07

I want to read your Thoughts

Are they of me
Are they of we
Are they of what we will some day be

Together forever with perfect love and perfect trust
For each night we share we will never have to lust

Lust for each other in the wee hours of the night
Both our hungers will be satisfied until daylight

I Want to Read Your Thoughts

Are they of me?
Are they of, we?
Are they of what we will someday be?

Together forever with perfect love and perfect trust
For each night we share we will never have to lust

Lust for each other in the wee hours of the night
Both our hungers will be satisfied until daylight

3/12/07

Curiousity

I'm curious to know what goes on in your mind
Does it wonder about what I'm doing at the time

I'm curious to know what exactly it is you love about me
On is it just the unreality and uncertainty of you and
I being a we

I'm curious to know where your heart will be without
me
Will it be trying to get back with your ex in hopes of
what used to be

I'm curious to know what goes through your mind
when I touch you
Does it make your total existence shiny and new on
frail and blue

I'm curious to know if you can handle my riding style
With such grace and poise and the distance of a
mile

I'm curious to know if you have the capabilities to
heal my soul
By pleasuring every ounce and inch of my body... fast
and slow

Curiosity

I'm curious to know what goes on in your mind
Does it wonder about what I'm doing at the time?

I'm curious to know what exactly it is you love about me
Or is it the unreality and uncertainty of you and I being a we

I'm curious to know where your heart will be without me
Will it be trying to get back with your ex in hopes of what used to be?

I'm curious to know what goes through your mind when I touch you
Does it make your total existence shiny and new or frail and blue?

I'm curious to know if you can handle my riding style
With such grace, poise, and the distance of a mile

I'm curious to know if you have the capabilities to heal my soul
By pleasuring every ounce and inch of my body, fast and slow

6/22/07

#1 Fan

I wish I could hear your voice
I wish you could hear mine

I wish I could hear what your heart is saying
I wish you could hear mine

I miss the scent of your cologne
I miss the strength of your hands
I miss the time we spend alone
I wish you ~~can~~ could just understand

Understand that I need you in my life
Understand that you are what makes me whole
Understand that I want to be your wife
And become one of two souls

I just wanted you to know that I'm your #1 fan!

#1 Fan

I wish I could hear your voice
I wish you could hear mine

I wish I could hear what your heart is saying
I wish you could hear mine

I miss the scent of your cologne
I miss the strength of your hands
I miss the time we've spent alone
I wish you could just understand

Understand that I need you in my life
Understand that you are what makes me whole
Understand that I want to be your wife
And become one of two souls

I just wanted you to know that I'm your #1 fan

Juvenile

Jealousy: Everything she has, I want but can't have; so I let it go. There's no more jealousy.

Unruly: A hard head makes a soft ass. But I'm not to be f**hed with

Vague: My life lacks so much shape but when I'm with you I have curves and meaning

Edgy: I tend to be this way when I can't get what I want, by writing "JUVENILE" letters

Negligent: Everything seems to always be about me so I forget who actually is supposed to matter

Impossible: Impossible is nothing but me

Livid: Is exactly how I get when I can't have my way

Effervescent: Is how I feel when I do get my way (devious smile)

Juvenile

Jealousy: Everything she has I want, but can't have; so I let it go.
  Then there's no more jealousy

Unruly: A hard head makes a soft ass. But I'm not to be f**ked with

Vague: My life lacks so much shape, but when I'm with you I have
  curves and meaning

Edgy: I tend to be this way when I can't get what I want, by writing
  "Juvenile" letters

Negligent: Everything seems to be always about me, so I forget who
  actually is supposed to matter

Impossible: Impossible is nothing but me

Livid: is exactly how I get when I can't have my way

Effervescent: Is how I feel when I do get my way (devious smile)

Mommie, Don't Go

I asked her a question
She told me no lie
The answer I will never mention
Assumed to be her destiny, it I will deny

Deny the fact that it's consuming my mother
Hide what it is that's making her so sick
I will not let this take the best of her
Then again, her future I cannot predict

I ask her, "Do you know where your destiny lies
Because what I said I do not want to come true"
She tells me, "This time I'm going to die."
I say, "I take it back, those words weren't meant for you"

The harshest thing I could have ever said
"This time you're going to die"
Those words I continue to dread
Please don't go yet, this is not the day nor the time

I'm haunted by the fear of you leaving this earth
Visions embedded in my mind of how you will go
How will I explain to my kids, who you are and what's
            your worth
I can't even pretend to have a clue, this I just don't know

So mommie please stay with me, don't go
I can't stop going through the motions and crying
I miss you more than these words could ever show
your love was snatched away so quick, now I'm dying

42

Mommie, Don't Go

I asked her a question
She told me no lie
The answer I will never mention
Assumed to be her destiny, it I will deny

Deny the fact that it's consuming my mother
Hide what it is that's making her so sick
I will not let this take the best of her
Then again her future I cannot predict

I ask her, "Do you know where your destiny lies?
Because what I said I do not want to come true"
She tells me, "This time I'm going to die!"
I say, "I take it back, those words weren't meant for you!"

The harshest thing I could have ever said
'This time you're going to die'
Those words I continue to dread
Please don't go yet, this is not the day, nor the time

I'm haunted by the fear of you leaving this earth
Visions embedded in my mind of how you will go
How will I explain to my kids, who you are and what's your worth
I can't even pretend to have a clue, this I just don't know

So mommie please stay with me, don't go
I can't stop going through the motions and crying
I miss you more than these words could ever show
Your love was snatched away so quick, now I'm dying

Dying to hear your voice
Dying to breathe your breath
Dying to hear, "I love you"
One last time before you rest

continued

Dying to hear your voice
Dying to breathe your breath
Dying to hear, 'I love you'
One last time before you rest

7/26/07

Mommie's Secret

She loves me
She loves me not
Does She
Or does she not

I think she does because she said so
But one can't go on by just that
I need to hear it, I need to feel it to know
Please tell me this isn't just another one of her acts

Acts of deceit to get what she wants
By verbalizing the word "love" to her prey
Falling deep into a trance and being emotionally drained
        of my thoughts
She disappoints me yet again, but on a different day

"Can you bring me some penny candy from the store?"
Is what I used to say
This request I knew she'd never ignore
Spellbound by the demands, now she is my prey

Mommie I know your secret
So you don't have to hide anymore
Tell me the truth, you wont regret it
Because I know what you're doing behind the
        bathroom door

46

Mommie's Secret

She loves me
She loves me not
Does she?
Or does she not?

I think she does because she said so
But one can't go on by just that
I need to hear it. I need to feel it to know
Please tell me this isn't just another one of her acts

Acts of deceit to get what she wants
By verbalizing the word, *'love'* to her prey
Falling deep into a trance and being emotionally drained of
my thoughts
She disappoints me yet again, but on a different day

"Can you bring me some penny candy from the store?"
Is what I used to say
This request I knew she'd never ignore
Spellbound by my demands, now she is my prey

Mommie, I know your secret
So you don't have to hide anymore
Tell me the truth, you won't regret it
Because I know what you're doing behind the bathroom door

47

The funnies of love ~~incompleted~~

The funniest thing about love is, that you never know how bad you're in it
Until you're up waiting for that person's call day in and day out and never get it

The funniest thing about love is, the other person will never know how you truly feel
Cause they take everything you say for granted so to them it's no big deal

The funniest thing about love is, you are willing to do anything for this person
But they fail to realize that you'd rather hurt than put their family through the motions

The funniest thing about love is, you tend to care a lot more then they ever will
Cause they think with the head between their legs not about how you really feel

11/7/08

The funniest thing about love, is, the other person
always ~~and~~ tells you how much they appreciate you
and what you do for them
But when its time to do for you, there's always
a ~~problem~~, ~~maybe~~ ~~maybe~~ I can't ~~or~~ I'll ~~try~~

      I'll try or I can't

11/5/07

48

The Funnies of Love

The funniest thing about love is, that you never know how bad you're
in it
Until you're up waiting for that person's call, day in and day out and
never get it

The funniest thing about love is, the other person will never know how
you truly feel
Cause they take everything you say for granted, so to them it's no
big deal

The funniest thing about love is, you are willing to do anything for
this person
But they fail to realize that you'd rather hurt than put their family
through the motions

The funniest thing about love is, you tend to care a lot more than they
ever will
Cause they think with the head between their legs, not about how you
really feel

The funniest thing about love is, the other person always tells you how
much they appreciate you and what you do for them
But when it's time to do for you, there's always a maybe, I'll try, or
I can't

Oct. 2007

Mother's
Through The ~~Parents~~ Eyes

When I was left alone in my shadow
Nothing and no one heard my soft sad sighs
My mood just a little too mellow
For only the heavens can hear my cry

The hardest decision I had to make
Was to decide between you and my own life
To God, my mother, my savior I prayed
Why must I be and feel so full of fright

So I mumble to myself time and time again
This wasn't the moment nor righteous way
To conceive a life and bring to an end
Now I suffer in the break of each day

I'm sorry for what had to come of this
I'm sorry for the pain I put you through
My unborn child I barely knew to even notice
Please forgive me for what I had to do

Forgive me for being so hasty, and not being still
I heard the words of the Lord, which I chose to ignore
Forgive me for not having faith on the power of will
To have you, hold you, cherish and adore

Understand that this was not your fault
As your father and I loved you very much
This was a lesson we had to learn and be taught
But what I wouldn't have given just to feel your
        touch

50

Through the Mother's Eyes

When I was left alone in my shadow
Nothing and no one heard my soft sad sighs
My mood just a little too mellow
For only the heavens can hear my cry

The hardest decision I had to make
Was to decide between you and my own life
To God, my mother, my savior I prayed
Why must I be and feel so full of fright

So I mumble to myself time and time again
This wasn't the moment nor righteous way
To conceive a life and bring to an end
Now I suffer in the break of each day

I'm sorry for what had to come of this
I'm sorry for the pain I put you through
My unborn child I barely knew to even miss
Please forgive me for what I had to do

Forgive me for being so hasty and not being still
I heard the words of the Lord which I chose to ignore
Forgive me for not having faith or the power of will
To have you, hold you, cherish, and adore

Understand that this was not your fault
As your father and I loved you very much
This was a lesson we had to learn and be taught
But what I wouldn't have given just to feel your touch

The touch of your little hand squeezing mine
Showing me how much you love me
Looking into your eyes and feeling our souls intertwine
What I wouldn't give to have heard your heart beat

Do you miss me?
Like I miss you
Do you forgive me?
For what I had to do

I'm afraid to die
Cause I fear going to hell
But I'd give anything to see you alive
And feel your warm body and inhale your baby smell

Every night I go to sleep
I look for you in my dreams
Curious to see if you like your daddy or me
Or like an angel of the heavenly beings

The touch of your little hand squeezing mine
Showing me how much you love me
Looking into your eyes and feeling our souls intertwine
What I wouldn't give to have heard your heart beat

Do you miss me
Like I miss you?
Do you forgive me
For what I had to do?

I'm afraid to die
Cause I fear going to hell
But I'd give anything to see you alive
And feel your warm body and inhale your baby smell

Every night I go to sleep
I look for you in my dreams
Curious to see if you look like your daddy or me
Or like an angel of the heavenly beings

Through The Unborn Child's Eyes

When you thought you were left alone in your shadow
And thought no one heard your soft sad sighs
Although your mood was just a little too mellow
I felt every single tear you cried

I thought I was an angel in disguise
Until the day you took that test
In less than a week, I came to realize
You keeping me wasn't in your best interest

I know it was a hard decision to make
For you to choose the destiny of my
To you, mother and father I prayed
Please don't fear me, I just want to see the light

The light of a new day
The warmth of this thing you call the sun
The night of that same day
Where I was thinking my life has just begun

I don't have to say to you time and time again
That what you contemplated on doing wasn't the righteous
     way
To conceive me and abruptly bring my life to an end
Why would you punish me for wanting to see the
     break of each day

I'm not sorry for what had to come of this
You have no idea the pain you put me through
Me, your unborn child you never wanted to exist
How can I forgive you for what you didn't have to
     do

54

Through the Unborn Child's Eyes

When you thought you were left alone in your shadow
And thought no one heard your soft sad sighs
Although your mood was just a little too mellow
I felt every single tear you cried

I thought I was an angel in disguise
Until the day you took that test
In less than a week I come to realize
You keeping me wasn't in your best interest

I know it was a hard decision to make
For you to choose the destiny of my life
To you, mother and father I prayed
Please don't fear me, I just want to see the light

The light of a new day
The warmth of this thing you call the sun
The night of that same day
Where I was thinking my life has just begun

I don't have to say to you time and time again
That what you contemplated on doing wasn't the righteous way
To conceive me and abruptly bring my life to an end
Why would you punish me for wanting to see the break of each day?

I'm not sorry for what had to come of this
You have no idea the pain you put me through
Me, your unborn child you never wanted to exist
How can I forgive you for what you didn't have to do?

I didn't think I'd ever cause you this much stress & strife
Perhaps you didn't love me enough or you were ashamed
I'm sure I wouldn't have brought harm to you or your
        "perfect" life
If it wasn't my fault, then who was to blame

Are you missing me?
Like I'm missing you
I so wish you believed in me
Like I trusted in you

Do not be afraid of dying
Cause I learned it is a part of life
I would much rather see you smiling
When you see me in the afterlife

Every night you go to sleep
No need to look for me in your dreams
Cause I look like you and my daddy
Keep looking in his eyes and you'll see what I mean

continued

I didn't think I'd ever cause you this much stress and strife
Perhaps you didn't love me enough or you were ashamed
I'm sure I wouldn't have brought harm to you or your "perfect" life
If it wasn't my fault then who was to blame

Are you missing me?
Like I'm missing you
I so wished you believed in me
Like I trusted you

Do not be afraid of dying
Cause I learned it is a part of life
I would much rather see you smiling
When you see me in the afterlife

Every night you go to sleep
No need to look for me in your dreams
Cause I look like you and my daddy
Keep looking in his eyes and you'll see what I mean

Missing Angel

I don't feel you're haunting me
But I do feel you're near
Your presence around me is so comforting
You were right, I have nothing to fear

Your heart, my heart, two hearts combined
Bound together by spirit, never to be brought down
I hope you never leave my side
As crazy as that may sound

I saw you in my dream last night
Even though you didn't come out of my belly
I knew it was you, the timing couldn't be more right
Cause when I touched you it seemed like you knew
me already

From your beautiful yellow skin
To your curly black hair
With the little clef in your chin
Yes we're two, but still one pair

Missing Angel

I don't feel you're haunting me
But I do feel you're near
Your presence around me is so comforting
You were right, I have nothing to fear

Your heart, my heart, two hearts combined
Bound together by spirit, never to be brought down
I hope you never leave my side
As crazy as that may sound

I saw you in my dream last night
Even though you didn't come out of my belly
I knew it was you, the timing couldn't be more right
Because when I touched you it seemed like you knew me already

From your beautiful yellow skin
To your curly black hair
With the little clef in your chin
Yes, we're two but still one pair

December '07'

MC Lovin

How do you let go of someone you've grown
to love so much
without trying to break their heart in the
knowing you're going to miss their scent and
the slightest hint of their touch
But you still try to let go because
you're obsessed

Obsessed with how he makes you feel
when he calls for a 2-minute talk
Obsessed with his erotic ~~the~~ sex appeal
Lovin' so good, you can hardly walk

You see what he does to ~~me~~ my psyche
Always making me go off the subject
~~from the taste of wine~~
To heal my soul, he does have the ability
Of his affection, I am the object

60

Me Lovin'

How do you let go of someone you've grown to love so much?
Without trying to break their heart in the process
Knowing you're going to miss their scent and the slightest hint of
their touch
But you still try to let go because you're obsessed

Obsessed with how he makes you feel
When he calls for a 2-minute talk
Obsessed with his erotic sex appeal
Lovin' so good you can hardly walk

You see what he does to my psyche
Always making me go off the subject
To heal my soul, he does have the ability
Of his affection, I am the object

What's next?
~~Never Satisfied~~

No matter what you have you'll always want more
more is what I don't want and not what I seek
So why do you always insist on knocking on that door
I'm sticking around to see if we are at all meant to be

I know I may be waisting my time
But 4 years is too much to just let go
For some reason I feel like you're only mine
However, I'm getting tired of just going w/the flow

The ups and downs, happiness & sadness
I can only imagine what true love must be like
I try hard everyday to keep my feelings suppressed
So tired, cause I feel like it's consuming my life

It is now day two since our last arguement
Two stubborn souls, how'd we ever get along
The exact thing we both tried to prevent
No calls, no emails, no communication at all

Tried to prevent being upset all the time
Over the simplest things that have logical explanations
But I'm not upset anymore after all this time
I'm just glad we came to a mutual revelation

What's Next?

No matter what you have you'll always want more
More is what I don't want and not what I seek
So why do you always insist on knocking on that door
I'm sticking around to see if we are at all meant to be

I know I may be wasting my time
But four years is too much to just let go
For some reason I feel like you're only mine
However, I'm getting tired of just going with the flow

The ups and downs, happiness and sadness
I can only imagine what true love must be like
I try hard every day to keep my feelings suppressed
So tired, cause I feel like it's consuming my life

It is now day two since our last argument
Two stubborn souls, how'd we ever get along?
The exact thing we both tried to prevent
No calls, no emails, no communication at all

Tried to prevent being upset all the time
Over the simplest things that have logical explanations
But I'm not upset anymore after all this time
I'm just glad we came to a mutual revelation

December '07
12/6/07

Letting Go

Do I miss you
Yea, I do
Can I live without you
As sure as the sky is blue

Since the day I met you
I knew this wouldn't last
Now that it's finally over between us two
I'm content enough not to go back

Letting Go

Do I miss you?
Yea I do
Can I live without you?
As sure as the sky is blue

Since the day I met you
I knew this wouldn't last
Now that it's finally over between us two
I'm content enough not to go back

12/19/07

Patience I.

Don't force it
It'll come naturally
Wait for it
And all its possibilities

Patience V.

Don't force it
It'll come naturally
Wait for it
And all its possibilities

12/20/07

Your Loss

I'm mad
I'm furious
Aren't you just a little curious

I hate you
you hate me
Don't you know we aint meant to be

The dirty dozens
Back and forth swearing
Don't you know I just aint carin'

This shit's for the birds
you're so not worth it
I just can't wait to make my exit

Out of this relationship
Out of your life
Cause I damn sure aint your wife

No way, no how
not gunna happen
Will I ever be an honest woman

68

Your Loss

I'm mad
I'm furious
Aren't you just a little curious?

I hate you
You hate me
Don't you know we aint meant to be?

The dirty dozens
Back and forth swearing
Don't you know I just aint carin'?

This shit's for the birds
You're so not worth it
I just can't wait to make my exit

Out of this relationship
Out of your life
Cause I damn sure aint your wife

No way, no how
Not gunna happen
Will I ever be an honest woman?

Honest with a ring
On the forbidden hand
Still can't be a man and take ~~a~~ that stand

Take a stand for what is right
Take a stand for what is true
It's either ~~me and you together~~ OR we're through

Well...time is now up
my love you did earn
However, someone else got your turn

continued

Honest with a ring
On the forbidden hand
Still can't be a man and take that stand?

Take a stand for what is right
Take a stand for what is true
It's either me and you or we're through

Well…time is now up
My love you did earn
However, someone else got your turn

12/22/07

Do me Right

like me
love me
Just don't hurt me

thrill me
excite me
Just don't spite me

Touch me
Take me
Just don't break me

caress me
and soothe me
Just don't use me

Do Me Right

Like me
Love me
Just don't hurt me

Thrill me
Excite me
Just don't spite me

Touch me
Take me
Just don't break me

Caress me
Soothe me
Just don't use me

12/22/07 ✓   Encouraged by Langston Hughes

Vain

(1) I'm not light skinned
(2) I'm light skinneded

(1) not as dark as you want me to be
(2) But damn if I aint fine as hell
(3) I'd like to think that I am a dime peice
(3) Beautiful complexion
(4) Perfectly complected

(The way I am is all pre-meditated)
(4) With just one glance, it aint hard to tell

(1) So I'm vain
(2) Yeah you think I am
(3) I'm ~~not~~ denying it
(4) Because I am', hot damn

1st   Red
2nd   Purple
3rd   blue

74

Vain

I'm not light skin
I'm light skinded
Beautiful complexion
Perfectly complected

Not as dark as you want me to be
But damn if I aint fine as hell
I'd like to think that I'm a dime piece
With just one glance, it aint hard to tell

So I'm vain
Yea…you think I am
I'm not denying it
Because I am…hot damn

12/23/07

Stubborn Mama

Please don't leave me
As you've done before
you've been given a second chance
And also a third and now a fourth

Why don't you value your life?
As much as I value you
I don't believe in this whole destiny thing
Because I know you can change it; if you really
wanted to

You are my mother
Make no mistake of that
But dammit if you aint stubborn
Stubborn as hell to be exact

76

Stubborn Mama

Please don't leave me
As you've done before
You've been given a second chance
And also a third, and now a fourth

Why don't you value your life?
As much as I value you
I don't believe in this whole destiny thing
Because I know you can change it, if you really wanted to

You are my mother
Make no mistake of that
But dammit if you aint stubborn
Stubborn as hell, to be exact

12/24/07 @ 12:13am

The Blame Game

You callin' me 'bout some damn guy
I don't wanna hear that shit
~~Instead call~~ ~~and ask me for my~~ help
Don't you know ~~cause~~ he's the one killing you
~~Also~~ Oblivious to what's going on, you can't even
see it

I wish I could hate him
① It's so easy to hate him
② for what he is doing to you
③ But should I really be hating him
for something you continue to do
④ Or should I be hating you

We share a heart and a soul
And of course, you know I could never hate you
I just want you to get better for yourself
And ~~tell~~ your grand-kids times two

The Blame Game

You callin' me bout some damn guy
I don't wanna hear that shit
Don't you know he's the one killing you?
Oblivious to what's going on, you can't even see it

It's so easy to hate him
For what he is doing to you
But should I really be hating him
Or should I be hating you?

We share a heart and a soul
And of course you know I could never hate you
I just want you to get better for yourself
And your grandkids, times two

12/24/07 @ 12:35am ✓

Love Conquers Addiction

That drug aint got nothing on us
or the love we have for you
you gotta have faith, believe in yourself & trust
That our love is stronger than anything, & it'll
pull you through

4 Through the urges you will get
\ Through the detoxing stage
2 Through the mid-night sweats
3 Through the feelings of being caged

Please don't give up on us
As we haven't given up on you
I say again, "That drug aint got nothing on us"
we can say it, but you have to feel it to be true

Love Conquers Addiction

That drug aint got nothing on us
Or the love we have for you
You gotta have faith, believe in yourself and trust
That our love is stronger than anything, and it'll pull you through

Through the detoxing stage
Through the midnight sweats
Through the feelings of being caged
Through the urges you will get

Please don't give up on us
As we haven't given up on you
I say again, that drug aint got nothing on us
We can say it, but you have to believe it to be true

12/24/07 @ 1:27 am

Survival through Song

One of the songs you used to sing me
I'm coming up... on the rough side... of the mountain
Creating everlasting memories of how things used to be
I'm doing my best..... to make it in

Heavily sedated, she won't remember a thing
Is what the dr's say you will not do
But as we all stand around your bed and sing
We know this you will remember to be true

True to your heart
from the love of your first born
Then the second and third heart
from the 4th, 5th & sixth born

from the first born nurturing two lives
Bet you thought the love ended with six
To the third born nurturing two lives
Bet you also thought the love wouldn't be infinite

82

Survival Through Song

One of the songs you used to sing to me
"I'm comin' up…on the rough side…of the mountain"
Creating everlasting memories of how things used to be
"I'm doin' my best, to make it in"

Heavily sedated, she won't remember a thing
Is what the doctors say you will not do
But as we all stand around your bed and sing
We know this you will remember to be true

True to your heart
From the love of your first born
Then the second and third heart
From the fourth, fifth and sixth born

From the first-born nurturing two lives
Bet you thought the love ended with six
To the third born nurturing two lives
Bet you also thought the love wouldn't be infinite

12/24/07 @ 1:40 am ✓

Time is of the Essence

Time will leave you
If you don't care about your life
Soon this devil will consume you
To where you can't put up a fight

Make a choice before it is too late
'Cause you're given another chance everyday
No one but you, can determine your own fate
So don't let fate determine you & take your life away

84

Time is of the Essence

Time will leave you
If you don't care about your life
Soon this devil will consume you
To where you can't put up a fight

Make a choice before it is too late
Cause you're given another chance everyday
No one but you can determine your own fate
So, don't let fate determine you and take your life away

12/24/07 @ 2:06 am
you Should Be Here

Where are you, when I need you?
working, trying to make ends meet
this bill, that bill, everything is overdue
no water, no lights and nothing to eat

How do you explain to a 4 year old
The actual value of a buck
When mommy & daddy can't give her anything cold
To soothe the bug bite on her foot

Every time she puts on a show
It's her way of camouflaging the pain
you think she has no idea and doesn't know
                    the ones
That mommy & daddy are to blame

"my daddy doesn't love me"
she said to me one day
Why do you say that baby? I asked ~~her immediately~~
~~No, that isn't true sweetheart~~
Because he's not here, he's far away

Oh no, that isn't true sweetheart
Your daddy loves you very much
            with you
He'd rather be out playing in the park
Enjoying your laugh giggle, smile and touch

86

You Should Be Here

Where are you when I need you?
Working, trying to make ends meet
This bill, that bill, everything is overdue
No water, no lights and nothing to eat

How do you explain to a 4-year old?
The actual value of a buck
When mommy and daddy can't give her anything cold
To soothe the bug bite on her foot

Every time she puts on a show
It's her way of camouflaging the pain
You think she has no idea and doesn't know
That mommy and daddy are the ones to blame

"My daddy doesn't love me"
She said to me one day
Why do you say that baby?
"Because he's not here, he's far away"

Oh no, that isn't true sweetheart
Your daddy loves you very much
He'd rather be out with you playing in the park
Enjoying your laugh, giggle, smile and touch

12/26/06 @ 9:42 pm ✓

Un-Supportive

I'm not supportive
How supportive do I have to be
I'm not supportive
When you won't even listen to me

I try to tell you something good
But I'm young so what do I know
I feel I'm being mis-understood
So now I think it's time for me to go

This doesn't mean I'm giving up on you
But our relationship has run it's coarse
I can't be with a man who still isn't true
And who's honestly I have to ply out with force

Do you know what I like?
Do you even care to know?
Because I like the simple things out of life
things you won't be around for me to show

88

Un-Supportive

I'm not supportive?
How supportive do I have to be?
I'm not supportive?
When you won't even listen to me

I try to tell you something good
But I'm young so what do I know
I feel I'm being misunderstood
So now I think it's time for me to go

This doesn't mean I'm giving up on you
But our relationship has run its course
I can't be with a man who still isn't true
And whose honesty I have to pry out with force

Do you know what I like?
Do you even care to know?
Because I like the simple things out of life
Things you won't be around for me to show

12/27/07 @ 8:25 pm   My Prerogative

Ask anyone too many questions
They'll ~~will~~ tell you at least 1 lie
No one is ever going to volunteer information
Go ahead and give it a try

My Prerogative

Are you gay?
I sure am
But in what way?
~~The~~ way your wouldn't understand

I like sex
But I'm not a nympho
what did you expect
from someone ~~this~~ so simple

                    lemme
Don't answer, ~~I'll~~ guess
        think
You ~~thought~~ I'm ~~was~~ a lesbian
Don't answer, lemme guess
                                    homosapien
you think of me not as a ~~human being~~

A lesbian I am .
And will forever be .
~~Make~~ Accept me as I am .
Cause I'm also gay ~~and truely happy~~
                    , yes.... I'm happy
                              very

90

My Prerogative I.

Are you gay?
I sure am
But in what way?
The way you wouldn't understand

I like sex
But I'm not a nympho
What did you expect?
From someone so simple

Don't answer, let me guess
You think I'm a lesbian?
Don't answer, let me guess
You think of me not as a homo sapien?

A lesbian I am
And will forever be
Accept me as I am
Cause I am also gay…yes, I'm very happy

12/27/07 @ 8:35 pm   ✓

MY PEROGATIVE II

You say it's not the Christian way
But I say people do it everyday

I am still your child
As you continue to be in denial

I never wanted anything from you
Except the occassional "I love you, too"

Is it too much to ask for
From the loving mother I've grown to adore

Wrap your arms around me tightly
Don't let go, squeeze with all your might

I know I put you through hours of labor
But this was all I ever wanted, and for to savor
              needed   long

might

92

My Prerogative VI.

You say it's not the Christian way
But I say people do it everyday

I am still your child
As you continue to be in denial

I never wanted anything from you
Except the occasional, *'I love you too'*

Is it too much to ask for?
From the loving mother I've grown to adore

Wrap your arms around me tight
Don't let go, squeeze with all your might

I know I put you through hours of labor
But this was all I've ever needed and longed for to savor

12/29/07 @ 8:56 pm

Suicide

you had such talent
why'd it go away?
you had such talent
why'd you end your life this way

After numerous attempts you never succeeded
Because I knew you had some sort of fear
But taking dose after dose; miligrams exceeded
The blurred vision I had of you is now clear

All the times I tried to help you
You knew all along what your plan was
feeling like the epitome of ridicule
You also knew that without me, there would
be no us

You're empty & you're drained
From life's bumps and bruises
No longer suffering from the pain
No longer here to make excuses

94

Suicide

You had such talent
Why'd it go away?
You had such talent
Why'd you end your life this way?

After numerous attempts you never succeeded
Because I knew you had some sort of fear
But taking dose after dose, milligrams exceeded
The blurred vision I had of you is now clear

All the times I tried to help you
You knew all along what your plan was
Feeling like the epitome of ridicule
You also knew that without me, there would be no us

You're empty and you're drained
From life's bumps and bruises
No longer suffering from the pain
No longer here to make excuses

12/30/07 @ 11:34 pm

Where's Daddy?

The last thing she says to me
Before closing those beautiful brown eyes
Then lays her head down to sleep
"my daddy don't ever come by"

So tired and delirious it comes out wrong
But I know exactly what she meant
She couldn't stay up and wait for daddy too long
But mommy is here, so therefore she's content

I hate to hear my baby girl say such things
Because I know exactly how one feels
However I never wanted her to experience these feelings
As I know it will ruin her, and take a long time to
heal

Where's Daddy?

The last thing she said to me
Before closing those beautiful brown eyes
Then lays her head down to sleep
"My daddy don't ever come by"

So tired and delirious it comes out wrong
But I know exactly what she meant
She couldn't stay up and wait for daddy too long
But mommy is here, so therefore she's content

I hate to hear my baby girl say such things
Because I know exactly how she feels
However, I never wanted her to experience these feelings
As I know it will ruin her and take a long time to heal

Happy thoughts

Happy thoughts, happy thoughts
whom ever came up with that slogan
"Think happy thoughts"
Had a serious anger problem

Happy Thoughts

Happy thoughts, happy thoughts
Whomever came up with that slogan
'Think happy thoughts'
Had a serious anger problem

1/3/08 @ 4:57 pm

Judge me not

The child
Do you dream?
If so, what are they about
Are things at all what they seem
Are all your dreams, filled with doubt

The mother
I stopped dreaming a long time ago
I don't think I even sleep anymore
steady scheming on ways to get my next blow
knocking at another crack house door

The mother
What I'm saying now, I could never tell to your face
Because I know what you must think of me
I'm so skinny & frail; to my family I'm of disgrace
So I ask that you please don't pass judgement, instead
accept my apology.

Judge Me Not

The Child:
Do you dream?
If so, what are they about?
Are things at all what they seem?
Are all your dreams filled with doubt?

The Mother:
I stopped dreaming long time ago
I don't think I even sleep anymore
Steady scheming on ways to get my next blow
Knocking at another crack house door

What I'm saying now I could never tell to your face
Because I know what you must think of me
I'm so skinny and frail, to my family I'm disgraced
So, I ask that you please don't pass judgment, instead accept
my apology

1/16/08 @ 1:05pm

Can't Get Right

I have a few more weeks in this place
And you still can't get things right while I'm here
I can't wait to get out and have my own space
So you can pull a houdini whenever you want and
disappear

One day you're hot and the next you're cold
I've grown so tired of this damn roller coaster
At what point do you stop and say, I'm getting too old
~~And then...~~
But still trying to be a bragger and a boaster

What's to brag about when you have nothing
And putting on a show to fake the funk
How about you get and earn that something
And discontinue the pursuit of this front

102

Can't Get Right

I have a few more weeks in this place
And you still can't get things right while I'm here
I can't wait to get out and have my own space
So you can pull a Houdini whenever you want and disappear

One day you're hot and the next you're cold
I've grown so tired of this damn roller coaster
At what point do you stop and say, 'I'm getting too old'
But still trying to be a bragger and a boaster

What's to brag about when you have nothing?
And putting on a show to fake the funk
How about you get and earn that something?
And discontinue the pursuit of this front

Be Firm

What are you doing
why are you back here again
He's only going to hurt you
Just like the others from way back when

If you stay you have to make it your duty
To maintain the upper hand
By standing firm by your decisions
And making him understand

Although you've got a good man
He is led by poor judgement
It won't be long before he strays
And you're back in the same predicament

If you're back for good
make sure this is what you want to do
Don't do it because of what people may say
Because the ultimate decision is up to you

104

Be Firm

What are you doing?
Why are you back here again?
He's only going to hurt you
Just like the others from way back when

If you stay you have to make it your duty
To maintain the upper hand
By standing firm by your decisions
And making him understand

Although you've got a good man
He is led by poor judgment
It won't be long before he strays
And you're back in the same predicament

If you're back for good
Make sure this is what you want to do
Don't do it because of what people might say
Because the ultimate decision is up to you

Tell me the Truth

I don't think ... ...
because you always pass your luck ... ...

I can ask a simple question and you'll tell me a lie
When I say I know the truth, that I'm sure you'll deny

If you love someone else, be man enough to tell me so
Don't let me find out what you think I'll never know

you're a charming, smooth talking man
To the extent I would never understand

you have a soft spot for people in need
Women with children to be exact ...... indeed

never took the time to think of how that makes me feel
Instead you take it as insecurity, uncertainty and unreal

How I feel is very real
Although to you, it may not appeal

Being that I know the truth it's a bit harder to let go
Cause I didn't think I'd find out so soon & feel this low

I wish I could erase from my thoughts, what I heard
Another woman saying she loves you; by this I'm very
disturbed

106

Tell Me the Truth

I can ask a simple question and you'll tell me a lie
When I say I know the truth; that I'm sure you'll deny

If you love someone else, be man enough to tell me so
Don't let me find out what you think I'll never know

You're a charming, smooth talking man
To the extent I will never understand

You have a soft spot for people in need
Women with children to be exact…indeed

Never took the time to think of how that makes me feel
Instead, you take it as insecurity, uncertainty and unreal

How I feel is very real
Although to you it may not appeal

Being that I know the truth it's a bit harder to let go
Cause I didn't think I'd find out so soon and feel this low

I wish I could erase from my thoughts what I heard
Another woman saying, she loves you, by this I am very disturbed

Deal With It

I don't think I'll ever look at men the same
Cause you always press your luck and play these games

you've tainted my thoughts of ever getting married
With the wicked traits in mind you carry

Just when I thought I loved you with all my heart
I don't think you were ever intended for me from the
start

you don't belong to me and I never belonged to you
So go be with your wife cause you and I are through

I know you don't like this cold side of me
But it's the harsh truth of this dryass Reality.

Deal with it!

108

Deal With It

I don't think I'll ever look at men the same
Because you always press your luck and play these games

You've tainted my thoughts of ever getting married
With the wicked traits in mind you carry

Just when I thought I loved you with all my heart
I don't think you were ever intended for me from the start

You don't belong to me and I never belonged to you
So go be with your wife because you and I are through

I know you don't like this cold side of me
But it's the harsh truth of this dry ass reality

Deal with it!

I miss us ✓

Soon there will come a day
Where I'll meet Mr. Right
Someone I can share my secrets with
From the rise of day to the dusk of night

I feel like I've found that person
cause he loves me, flaws and all
But I can't be with him like I want to
As he alters my perception and clouds X my thoughts

I get annoyed when I don't hear from him
Like he's not answering my calls on purpose
Then again I don't care right (not)
But I am going to miss him and I being an us

I Miss Us

Soon there will come a day
Where I'll meet Mr. Right
Someone I can share my secrets with
From the rise of day to the dusk of night

I feel like I've found that person
Because he loves me, flaws and all
But I can't be with him like I want to
As he alters my perception and clouds my thoughts

I get annoyed when I don't hear from him
Like he's not answering my calls on purpose
Then again, I don't care right (not)
But I am going to miss, him and I being an us

Same Color in The Dark

He is of another race
And of a different creed
With Angel-like eyes on his flawless face
And a smile that has Rendered me speechless, indeed

The act of pursuing him has crossed my mind
But I don't know how he feels about my type
Dumb-struck by the age and nature of my kind
I'm sure he's curious to know as well what I'm like

112

Same Color in the Dark

He is of another race
And of a different creed
With angel-like eyes on his flawless face
And a smile that has rendered me speechless, indeed

The act of pursuing him has crossed my mind
But I don't know how he feels about my type
Dumb struck by the age and nature of my kind
I'm sure he's curious to know as well what I'm like

His Insecurity

While I'm rich on personality
you're insane on insecurity

You always get the wrong impression
Because you think everyone craves your obsession

An innocent hello from me
To you determines my availability

Why can't you see things my way
Or discontinue this pursuit, if you may

His Insecurity

While I'm rich on personality
You're insane on insecurity

You always get the wrong impression
Because you think everyone craves your obsession

An innocent hello from me
To you, determines my availability

Why can't you see things my way?
Or discontinue this pursuit if you may

Too Little, Too Late

(4) I love you enough now, to hate you later
(1) The things I've always wanted but couldn't get
(2) you now want to provide it, and supposedly cater
(3) Soon I will have no need or want for you, just regret

you claim to love me but you have yet to show
maybe it'll surface when I'm two-steps out the door
By that time you would have lost that glow
The glow that has always kept me coming back for more.

116

Too Little, Too Late

The things I've always wanted but couldn't get
You now want to provide it and supposedly cater
Soon I will have no need or want for you, just regret
I love you enough now to hate you later

You claim to love me, but you have yet to show
Maybe it'll surface when I'm two-steps out the door
By that time you would have lost that glow
The glow that has always kept me coming back for more

Hell-crazy love

I'm not gone yet
But damn if it don't hurt like hell, crazy
Though this feeling is to be expected
I'm going to miss you so much boy, baby

You got me all twisted
As I keep using one word too much, many
To you I may appear to be gifted
But to me I just have a lot to say, plenty

Are you going to miss me
As much as I will miss you like hell, crazy
Only time will tell and we shall see
If we were at all meant to be boy, baby

118

Hell-Crazy Love

I'm not gone yet
But damn if it don't hurt like hell-crazy
Though this feeling is to be expected
I'm going to miss you so much boy-baby

You have me all twisted
As I keep using one word too much-many
To you I appear to be gifted
But to me I just have a lot to say-plenty

Are you going to miss me?
As much as I miss you like hell-crazy
Only time will tell and we shall see
If we were at all meant to be boy-baby

The Distance I.

This was supposed to be a good move
But I find myself feeling lonely at night
It's only been a week, perhaps I should give it a chance
yea that's what I'll do and I should be alright

But I'm not cause I miss you
like hell crazy, boy baby.

120

The Distance I.

This was supposed to be a good move
But I find myself feeling lonely at night
It has only been a week, perhaps I should give it a chance
Yea, that's what I'll do and I should be alright

But I'm not, because I miss you like hell crazy…boy baby

2/11/08

Confessedly

I've always loved you
Just had the worst way of showing it
you deserve to be happy

If she is what you want...
Then by all means...

I'll discontinue the confessions of
my feelings and spare you
the all day fulfillments of confusion

122

Confessedly

I've always loved you
Just had the worst way of showing it
You deserve to be happy

If she is what you want
Then by all means…

I'll discontinue the confessions of my feelings
And spare you the all day fulfillment of confusion

Don't Be...

Don't be sad
Don't be mad
As you got what you wished for

Don't be sad
Don't be mad
As you've had your chance before

Don't be sad
Don't be mad
As he loved you from the start

Don't be sad
Don't be mad
As all you had to do was open your heart

Don't be sad
Don't be mad
If someone else has captured his eye

Don't be sad
Don't be mad
As your time came, went and has now gone by

124

Don't Be...

Don't be sad
Don't be mad
As you've got what you wished for

Don't be sad
Don't be mad
As you've had your chance before

Don't be sad
Don't be mad
As he loved you from the start

Don't be sad
Don't be mad
As all you had to do was open your heart

Don't be sad
Don't be mad
If someone else has captured his eye

Don't be sad
Don't be mad
As your time came, went and has now gone by

karma

Does he still have a soft spot for you
or has it gone away, onto someone new

She doesn't love him like I do
This I feel is a fact and is true

Although everything is repairable
This time I don't think it's doable

My past has come back to haunt me
now it's time I ride out this thing against me

This thing that won't go away overnight
This thing that's taken me by force I might

This thing that is very much known of
This thing we all consider to be, "karma"

126

Karma

Does he still have a soft spot for you?
Or has it gone away onto someone new

She doesn't love him like I do
This I feel is a fact and is true

Although everything is repairable
This time I don't think it's doable

My past has come back to haunt me
Now it's time I ride out this thing against me

This thing that won't go away overnight
This thing that's taken me by force and might

This thing that is very much known of
This thing we all consider to be karma

✓ She's not your Type

I'll keep my distance for now
Just as you asked me to
But you make it so hard to do when you're around
As all I want to do is tell you I love you

There's that word love again
Have you asked her what it is she loves about you
Which Brings me to my next question
Does she ask the same thing to you

If you choose to be with her
I have no other choice but to accept it
However I am going to miss the way we were
And the good things we did out of habit

She may have more money than me
But she is lacking something inside
I'm hoping and praying that you can see
That she doesn't love you half as I

She's Not Your Type

I'll keep my distance for now
Just as you asked me to
But you make it so hard to do when you're around
As all I want to do is tell you I love you

There's that word *love* again
Have you asked her what it is she loves about you?
Which brings me to my next question?
Does she ask the same thing to you?

If you choose to be with her
I have no other choice but to accept it
However, I am going to miss the way we were
And the good things we did out of habit

She may have more money than me
But she is lacking something inside
I'm hoping and praying that you can see
That she doesn't love you half as I

Say you, say me

Say me:

I just had a preminition
About what you said to me earlier
I think I might of come to the realization
That you do in fact want to be with her

Say you:

Focus on yourself
And stop worrying about my decision
Focus on yourself
And look within your soul for a vision

Say me:

By you telling me this
you've already given me your answer
I guess in your heart, I'm officially dismissed
I'm gracefully bowing out while you pursue her

P.S. I've always loved you...
(I admit) Just had the worst way of shaying it...
You deserve to be happy...
if she is what you want...
then so am I this.
I'll descontinue the content
of my feelings and spare you
the all day fulfilment of confusion.

130

Say You, Say Me

Say me:
I just had a premonition
About what you said to me earlier
I think I might have come to the realization
That you do in fact want to be with her

Say you:
Focus on yourself
And stop worrying about my decision
Focus on yourself
And look within your soul for a vision

Say me:
By you telling me this
You've already given me your answer
I guess in your heart I'm officially dismissed
I'm gracefully bowing out while you pursue her

Patience II.

This feeling's so strange
I can't be myself around you
Everything was so abruptly rearranged
I don't know what's the next best thing to do.

I used to be the chase
now I'm the chaser
I so wish this wasn't the case
so I don't want to end up the loser

Losing is a state of mind
what is meant for you
will be yours in time

Patience VI.

This feeling's so strange
I can't be myself around you
Everything was so abruptly rearranged
I don't know what's the next best thing to do?

I used to be the chase
Not I'm the chaser
I so wish this wasn't the case
As I don't want to end up the loser

Losing is a state of mind
What is meant for you
Will be yours in time

Acknowledgements

First and foremost, I'd like to thank God for giving me the guidance and strength to follow my heart and be able to boldly express my passion poetically to the world. Through you all things are possible.

Thank you, husband, for believing in me, helping, and pushing me to bring this project into fruition. I love that you continue to encourage and empower me to express my craft without judgement and remain secure in our relationship. I am grateful to you for being my bestie!

Thank you to my son and daughter for being the balance and beauty in my life. You continue to make me a proud mom every day.

Thank you to my author friend for the constant nudge over the years and interest in wondering when Ciara is going to make her poetic debut.

Thank you to everyone who has purchased my book and can relate to these experiences. Stay tuned for *ORGANIC*, book #2 of this poetic journey!

About the Author

Photo by Jason Cordes Photography

Ciara Dove was born and raised in Passaic, New Jersey. She is the third child on her mother's side and one of many siblings on her father's side. In 1995, her literature teacher told her she had great writing skills which empowered Ciara with a passion for writing. While she did take a hiatus from writing, in 2006 she felt as though inspiration reignited in her soul and she wrote over 300 poems.

facebook.com/AuthorCiaraDove/

TikTok: @authorciaradove

Milton Keynes UK
Ingram Content Group UK Ltd.
UKHW020619191223
434598UK00002B/28